TOGETHER, WE CAN DO IT

by Shashi Patel

Orlando Boston Dallas Chicago San Diego

Visit *The Learning Site!*

www.harcourtschool.com

People work together to help their communities. Some people become volunteers or join community groups. Volunteering is a great way to spend free time. When you volunteer, you spend special time with friends and family. You learn more about your community, learn new skills, and help others.

Volunteering also can prepare you for the kind of work you might want to do as an adult. For example, if you want to work with animals, you could learn a lot more by volunteering at a zoo or animal shelter. There are so many ways to work together!

Neighborhood Projects

There are opportunities to help in most neighborhoods. If you look around and talk to people, you will see things that can be done. Sometimes there are people who are unable to do work on their homes. They might need help painting, or they might need help fixing things around the house. Volunteers can help these people. Community efforts to paint and fix homes for people are a great way to work together to help others.

Some communities have special days to help citizens with the care of their homes. Volunteer groups find the homes that need work, and they make plans to help. These groups then find people willing to give time and effort. Everyone is part of a team. Every team has a leader. Volunteers may be members of churches, local businesses, or neighbors on your street. Everyone helps and everyone benefits.

Another type of neighborhood project is a community garden. Being part of a community garden project is fun, and there is much to learn. Some volunteer groups plant vegetable gardens to grow food.

Some groups plant community flower gardens for everyone to enjoy. Vacant lots and fields are good places to plant gardens. Volunteer groups usually work with the community to decide where to put a garden. People in the community will sometimes lend tools and other supplies to make the project a success.

Clean and Safe Parks

Parks are important parts of many towns and cities. Most towns and cities have parks. Some parks provide places to sit and places to play tennis, basketball, and other games. Other parks have historical features and monuments. These parks need to be cared for.

Volunteers can help take care of the parks. Volunteers can pick up garbage, plant trees, and fix and paint old equipment. There are many things to do to improve parks. There are groups who want to help, and they always need volunteers.

Beaches, Rivers, and Lakes

It is important for people to care for parks. Parks need to be kept clean and safe. There are other places that need volunteer help, too. Beaches, rivers, and lakes are places where volunteers can help. Communities along the ocean often need volunteers to help clean up beaches. Beaches become dirty as more and more people use them. Volunteers can help by being a part of programs that tell people how litter harms the beach.

Like the beach, rivers and lakes get dirty, too. Sometimes garbage gets washed into a river or lake after a rain storm. Volunteer groups schedule special cleanup events to help protect rivers and lakes.

Teams of volunteers walk along the river to pick up garbage. Sometimes volunteers can use canoes to pick up garbage as they paddle down the river.

Places Near You

Besides cleaning, gardening, and painting, communities need help in other ways. Many community and city workers welcome volunteers.

Groups can work with the community to create safety programs. Volunteers can work with the community to help create programs to find missing children. There also are projects where volunteers can repaint buildings that are covered in graffiti. There are many ways volunteers can help people who help the community.

There are other places in the community where volunteers can help. Some groups go to senior citizens centers. Many senior citizens enjoy having visitors. Volunteers of all ages can spend time with older people. Together they can read, talk, or play games. They may go to the movies or to a park. Some volunteers will teach senior citizens how to use computers to help them check out library books, send e-mail, and find information.

Volunteers can help at other places in the community, too. Local libraries are always in need of books and other resources. Volunteers can support libraries by doing many things. There are volunteers who participate in one-time events. There are volunteers who give their time on a regular basis.

Many people can give books and magazines to their library. Libraries in large cities have programs to help people learn to read. Young people help out in libraries by volunteering to put away books or by reading to younger children.

Helping Animals

Zoos, animal parks, and animal shelters always need help from volunteers. There are a lot of animals in a zoo, and there is much to do. The zookeepers need people who want to care for animals. Animals need to be fed and cleaned. Zookeepers also need help with special programs that teach visitors about different kinds of animals.

Animal parks are places where animals are kept for protection and study. Volunteers in some programs can take part in the daily activities of these parks. Volunteers can work with the visitors and learn about the feeding and care of some wild animals.

Local animal shelters need help from community members. They have so many animals that need homes. These shelters need people to help care for the animals by feeding and playing with them. They need volunteers to help with pet adoption programs so the animals can go to good homes. They need volunteers to educate the community and to tell others about pets for adoption. Animals need volunteer help, too!

Raising Money

Sometimes people raise money. These volunteers raise money to help groups and community members who need it. Community volunteers can hold bake sales to raise money for schools and libraries. Young people can wash cars to make money for schools, new park equipment, gardens, and other community centers.

Another way to raise money is to have a community yard sale. People sell things they no longer need. Then they give away the money they make.

Raising money is a great way to be involved in a community project. Volunteers can play a role in doing something helpful for others. They also get a chance to learn more about the people where they live.

Community volunteers are needed for many things. They clean, paint, plant gardens, take care of people and animals, and they raise money. There are many more things community volunteers can do, too. Volunteers can help people in other communities and in other countries. Volunteers see problems and then work together to solve those problems.

Volunteers come from all age groups. Young people can be a great help whether they are volunteering with their parents or by themselves. Whatever the cause, volunteers make a difference.